G000060380

WOMAN'S HEAD AS JUG

WOMAN'S
HEAD AS JUG
Jackie Wills

PUBLICATIONS
2013

Published by Arc Publications
Nanholme Mill, Shaw Wood Road
Todmorden OL14 6DA, UK
www.arcpublications.co.uk

Design by Tony Ward
Printed in Great Britain by the
Berforts Information Press Ltd.

978 1906570 83 5 (pbk)
978 1906570 84 2 (hbk)
978 1908376 29 9 (ebook)

Cover image:
The Five Sisters of Suduireaut by Jane Sybilla Fordham,
by kind permission of the artist.

Editor for UK & Ireland: John W. Clarke

AUTHOR'S ACKNOWLEDGEMENTS

I would like to thank the editors of the following publications in which some of the poems in this collection have appeared: *Agenda, Dark Horse, Molossus World Poetry Series, Poetry Wales, The Echo Room* and *Warwick Review.*

My thanks go to Jane Sybilla Fordham for the title, 'Woman's head as jug' and for her prints, drawings and paintings that live within these poems. Her work has never illustrated mine, my poems have never been about her work, but we have been writing and drawing together since 2006 often using the same sources, so we are true collaborators. Thanks also to David Parfitt for encouraging us.

I am grateful to Moniza Alvi, Martha Kapos, Christina Dunhill, Kate Smith-Bingham, and Susan Wicks – my London lifeline – who've read many of these poems, as well as Maria Jastrzębska, Robert Hamberger, Lee Harwood, John McCullough, Janet Sunderland, Bernadette Cremin and Robert Dickinson – the Brighton gang, or as John O'Donoghue calls us, the Beach Generation. For reminding me what it's all about, as always my thanks go to Brendan Cleary, Catherine Smith, Lorna Thorpe and Michael Hulse.

I am indebted to the Royal Literary Fund for Fellowships at Surrey and Sussex universities.

Finally, I would like to thank my mum Sheila Alcock and my children Mrisi and Giya.

CONTENTS

I

II

III
SWEATS

IV

I

A LONE LEAPING WOMAN*

doesn't leave a crater

landless – she picks up days
of work like kindling

only the river curves
around her shoulders

OWNER OF A MANGLE

I wind patchwork sheets into a tub
flatten nights between rollers

smoother for the sleeping bodies
passing through, long and thin

these sheets are for the wind
its pollen and its emptiness

* Itinerant female labourer, mediaeval England.

13

FEATHER-WIFE

I wash blood from every kind of plume,
remove skin from the quill,

I sell them clean –
in shades of white and grey,

green black, purple black.
When I smooth a yellow edge

I see the death
of flight, the robin's chest.

I pack in boxes what a wing remembers
of the river, a hill's lurch,

the wren's nest inside a skull.
I layer them with songs,

notes clinging to a branch.
My smallest feather brushes

the draught of a continent
across your cheek.

For a hat, I burn a pheasant tail
into curls, pluck mallard's wings –

run the knowledge of a river
through an umber field.

SATURDAY GIRL

When the power was cut in 1974
the manager lit candles. We carried fabric
to the door for customers to check in daylight.
I learned crepe and twill – my hands explored
the dark for taffeta and gauze. All I earned, I spent.
Browsing pattern books I learned to clothe myself
by knowing nap and seam allowance, how to cut
a yoke on the bias. Start with Simplicity, progress

to Vogue. I thought I was choosing well, an easy tunic
in Liberty Varuna wool – clumps of red flowers on black.
I unravelled the bolt, measured each yard against a brass rule.
The manager handed me scissors. I was afraid to cut.
She snipped the selvedge for me, guided the blade,
wrapped in paper the dress I never finished and still crave.

GRACE-WIFE*

When she growls, it starts –
morning still so far below
and her husband outside
listening until his eyes are red.

* Midwife

15

HERRING GIRL

And as the fish rise to the surface
the water fires with Gaelic songs.

The shoal is eight miles long
and four miles wide. A fleet of drifters

pulls in sheets and sheets of silver
five thousand of us, knife sharp,

on the quayside. I sing
to stand the pain of salt, of men

and herring that escape the nets
carry my songs to sea again,

cast them back as blackthorn flowers
in the spring.

DORSET BUTTONMAKER

The first stitch, after laying,
runs from east to west,
the second north to south,

until the small moons fastening
your collar and both cuffs
are done. This is a honeycomb,

but not a bee's. Here's a cartwheel
that won't carry hay. The bird's eye
sees nothing beyond me –

my thread filling a circle
of horn, the silence between
my needle and thumb.

BLACKSMITH

I made a pillow out of iron, a pair of shoes,
I made a tutu, my mother's hat,
iron lashes for my eyes, iron fingernails,
I made myself a bridle and a belt.

I made a baby out of iron, I hammered out
a tree in bud, a nest of yellow beaks.
I smelted, riveted, cast my hands
into bellows. I blew a cumulus of sparks –

they found the corners of a room,
a hidden silhouette, they settled
on a dusty charcoal bed
and from the shadows made a forge.

CORSET-MAKER

What do you want girl
between your breasts
and jutting hips – a ravine, a cutting,

or a valley's slopes?
Soft stays that work like muscle
or a harness made of steel, bone?

FRIPPERER

I grope the impossible pile of clothes,
unleash armpits, urine, cigarettes.

People throw out shirts for want of a button.
I hunt silk, lambswool, linen – they sell.

But this cashmere's mine. It holds me in,
pours me into a moss garden so soft

I can unlace my painful shoes at last.

BOARDING HOUSE KEEPER

They share a bed mid journey
like horses between home and somewhere else.

I've seen them unload lives,
a silver cross, bottle of perfumed oil.

Some have nothing to put beside them.

ALE-WIFE

He turns on a gulp,
his mouth opening
once too often,

and I'm the strum, venturer,
a night-worm
for his empty palm.

But this one talks to me
as if I'm a girl in a field
he rowed to under bridges

glimmering with a canal
stopped at midsummer.
He puts each coin

on the bar so carefully,
sliding me the gold of a day
he replays and replays.

II

FOREST CHOIR

She's in that old light again,
inventing sleep without sirens,
the first blackbird cutting through the blinds.

Hunters, mushroom gatherers,
woodsmen pass by the door
to a thrush's trio of notes.

She hears the robin
summon water from rock,
the wagtail raise islands with its wings.

Days without sun –
hail splits the seam
between June and December.

Her heart opens its sluice gates.
Her lungs gulp hurricanes.
A wren fills the forest where nothing else sings.

She stares into a fire
willing sparks to make a bridge
between earth and sky.

Night senses the hollows she's slept in.
If she's still
it will eat from her hand.

She asks the gale to deliver
a gorse yellow slope, call seals
into a bay, bring her a boat.

In the space an axe makes,
the tree's retina, charcoal heart,
she smells blackcurrants.

The forest sings to her
of cures,
of its flutes, auricles, air-roots.

She's listening for orchids,
asking the sun to return a footprint
forgotten on a rock.

She'll assemble her lover from willow,
blackthorn, alder, fingers of yew,
cherry, lime, copper beech.

The forest sings to her of a headland,
the crunch of a boat on gravel,
a path wrapped into night.

Once she was a hermit, a schooner,
a logger's blaze, the Cloud Forest,
both kelp and rowan – the famine tree.

There's salt in her throat,
a gossip of crows,
a tray full of smoke.

Beneath the sapling are turquoise clay pits,
an Assyrian priest,
his fish head, his glinting cloak.

In the centre of the forest
a dark star spits webs, ant runs,
honeycomb.

She'll return the shadows she made
to the sea. Only waves
can do anything useful with them.

In the groves and their silences,
trees capture each second
the clock sheds.

The forest sings to her
of abandoned altars,
of its scaled and feathered beginning.

WORDS FOR WOMEN

AMAZONAUNTADULTERESSASSBEAV
ERBITCHBIRDBABYBAWDBALLBREA
KERBAGGAGEBLUESTOCKINGBIDDIE
BIMBOBINTBRIDEBROADCOQUETTEC
ATCHARCHICKCUNTCONSORTCOWC
OMPANIONCONCUBINECOURTESANC
HATELAINECRONEDEBDONNADOOL
ADISTAFFDAMSELDAMEDELILAHDIV
ADISHDOWAGERDOXYDOLLDIVORC
EEEXENCHANTRESSEMPRESSFEMAL
EFIANCEEFOXFRAUFEMINISTFLAGFL
APPERFLIRTFLOOZYFUSBYGALGEISH
AGIRLGRAVIDAGOLDDIGGERGODDE
SSHENHEIFERHUSSYHAGHAYBAGHA
RRIDANHONEYHEROINEHOURIHARL
OTINAMORATAJEZABELJULIEJUDYJU
GJADEKITTENLOVERLADYLASSLUBR
ALOOKERLESBOLESBIANLULUMOTH
ERMISTRESSMISSUSMATEMATRONM
ATRIARCHMEOWLEMINXMAIDMAEN
ADMAREMANIKINMILFMADONNAMA
DAMMUFFMAREMOLLMESTIZANANN
UMBERNURSENULLIPARANYMPHNIE
CEPARTNERPLACKETPARTLETPOON
ANGPRINCESSPROSTITUTEPETTICOA
TPERIWINKLEPIECEPINTAILPUSSYPO
PSYPOTATOPRICKTEASEQUEENQUIM
QUAILRAGAMUFFINRUNNIONROWEN
SIRENSKIRTSPOUSESTOTSTUNNERSIS
TERSWEETHEARTSWOPSONSQUEEZE
SMOCKSPLITSHEILASHIKSASTRAPSO
WSUGARSHREWSTRUMPETSKIRTSUL
TANASYLPHTARTTITTOTTYTEMPTRE
SSTIGRESSTROUTTOOTSIEVIXENVAM
PVIRAGOVIRGINWHOREWAREWIFMA
NNWITCHWENCHWIFEWIDOWWREN

WOMAN'S HEAD AS JUG

after a title by Jane Fordham

Today she pours the Water of Life – green
walnuts picked in June, beaten with a pestle.

Tomorrow, Melancholy Water tasting of gilliflower,
damask rose, musk and gold leaf.

She steeps pounds of rue for Plague Water,
and to clear 'mists and clouds of the head'

infuses peacock dung and bruised millipedes
in spirit of lavender. Bending over a bowl

she might empty a reservoir, reveal the valley it invaded.
Her head is fired from the same earth.

CLIFF

Paths head to the edge, away,
an escarpment widens to the sea,

there's an ochre band, a green top,
shadows that could be caves,

shrines the sea makes out of faults
and cloisters where shadows chant

menus for the week, the rapid dawn,
cricket-note afternoons.

It filters all I'm thinking,
takes me to its heart and holds me there.

LA FONTASSE

There are so many bends in the stone track through the maquis,
we walk past myrtle, sage and juniper – no evidence of the place.
We don't know what to expect until it's in front of us –
a low yellow house, hiding in a sweltering afternoon.

There's a man on a porch playing chess with the view
and Jean-Pierre, who shows us the tap. Tomorrow we'll swim
and watch boys fly from a fingernail of rock
into water so clear nothing could ever be lost.

CALANQUE

I took breaths,
dipped my head underwater –

they were feeding
in the seagrass meadow,

fifty at least,
silver, black and yellow,

tipped at 30 degrees,
mouths to the weed,

the calanque pale turquoise,
lit with rods of sun.

The rest of the shoal
surrounded me, swam on

and I drifted with them
until they made a column

to graze at the surface –
each fish waiting its turn.

Later, the moon filled the bay,
threw itself into the water,

forcing everything to overflow.
I watched from the wall,

so heavy again, the shoal
quickening far below.

FIREWORKS ON THE FEAST OF THE ASSUMPTION

The sky's turned to water,
the day-old sturgeon moon stays the same.

But what are the tides of air doing
and what's in the gunpowder

that makes jellyfish surge towards us
over the maquis – absorbing me,

enthralling you? Me under the vine
and you next to the young olive tree.

THE SEALS' GOODBYE

His kisses, soft as anemones, dab liner from my cheeks.
The train rolls out, imperceptibly.

It's too soon to stop, wrong, a backward look,
when I'm still chanting Sanctus to the rocks.

Evolution with all its blunders made the eye
and everything it sees: a salty bed, the seals' goodbye.

MACKEREL SHOAL

The sea boiled with mackerel
inches from the shore –

it was thundery, a glassy July evening,
gulls dived, boys ran shouting with rods.

The shoal had followed her
from a darker, granite coast, hard with snow.

Boys cast lines sparkling with lures,
the beach twitched with blue-grey piles

that turned silver and still and a boat slowed
its engine. Everything was changed.

HER YEAR

Winter

a goose duck mallard pheasant
teal partridge pigeon plover
lapwing quail thrush lark
bunting and lastly a warbler

               lie inside a swan

a bell hangs from the beak of its severed head

she scratches a calendar line by line

    *

snow has settled inside her
the vixen, rabbit and their journeys
will last long after it thaws

    *

the moon this morning is pinned to a horizon
the colour of crab apple jelly –

new, thin… she looks up and it's gone

Spring

she misses her children's hands
the chiff-chaff when it arrives
only repeats its own name

*

she's going to dress the scarecrow
in Jenny Barelegs' field

put her in a red taffeta dress
with velvet round the neck

from a distance
she'll see herself as she was

flashing a necklace of CDs
skirt blown into a dance

*

she feels the first line
burned on her back
from an afternoon sowing seeds

Summer

when those thirteen days quivered
her flesh was a hammock

she looped herself from the Pavilion scaffolding
filled an arch in the viaduct

every sound the baby heard through its skin wall
was suspended between loitering seconds

*

she follows a wall underground
to palaces, mosaics, markets, crossroads
where people ate, shouted over thunder

*

daring herself to climb a beech
she heaves her body into a V
leaves applaud
she makes herself invisible in the canopy

must learn to live alone

in a distant city sycamores pierce office roofs
the tree creaks
she hears joists intoning the questions
she once asked a mirror

Autumn

she was trying to keep up
with a glut of beans
and counting between pains
her second baby was fast

slept among pumpkins
and coaxed mushrooms
put a reed to its mouth
found a note

*

by a soot-stained fireplace
she counts yellow kayaks
back into the fan they moored in

*

she's bled into the red sofa
her best underwear
two seasons of cherry blossom

a Chanel lipstick   post-boxes
Valentine hearts   hand-fired bricks
and everything's sodden

TRANSLATIONS FROM THE SILENCE OF COLOUR

1

Even red, first and loudest, is silenced
as it totters into cornfields and flirts,
as it murmurs and smudges,
shelters under the rock
grunting words for deer, stream, placenta.

From somewhere in the mess of a peony
collapsed on a table, from veins in an eye,
the tip of a tampon, a sore and a crater,
red is smeared with its own absence:
what remains when there's no skin to paint on?

2

It roughens your tongue and roof of your mouth,
sleepy in the afternoon,
limb wrapped around limb.

At times when green enters your eyes
it won't leave.
It sends out echoes endlessly,

travels down the centre of roads,
bends over them,
turns them to jade.

It flares, but its great inland seas part
for anything tracing straight lines – a lorry or a cat.
It shields the cub in its den.

3

So hard fought for, ground, boiled, simmered, left to ferment,
it's the hum or reed in your ear, a string picked steadily.

From morning glory to a vein enlarged by heat
it's drawn to mist, deflects your eye to space leaking into a wood.

Blue's always in your mind

when you look up from a job,
when your head tilts in its cup.

4

Drink, drink, drink the desert and sunflower field,

there's never enough,
urine yellow, the nearly gold
of feathers and fins.

Yellow boasts its elaborate gateposts
arrows of sun.

5

Disappearing tail,

white doesn't exist. It does exist.
It belongs to sky, to earth…
to sky, no, to earth.

6

Your pupil is drawn into a hole,
cell after cell,
all the rooms you lived in,
sucked into a Dyson,
one containing rosary beads, another willows by the stream.

Black pulls you to the seabed head first,
your fists around a rope, air strapped to your back.
Breathe through your mouth. Trust your hands.

CANOPY

When boots left the path
in that forest,
the canopy hushed.

Each tree held back light,
mote by mote.
Ants stripped the bones.

The city creeps
up mountainsides
towards distant, painted shrines.

Thorns whiffle with ribbon,
a newborn's sock,
a doll's lace bra.

BALANCE

Did an alarm
bleep unnoticed

when the years I had left
were equal to those I'd lived,

when past and future
were as balanced

as a chunk of butter
and a four ounce weight?

MOULTS

When she moulted the first time,
        she thought she'd found a missing twin –
but her seven-year-old skin buried itself

in the roots of their cherry tree.
        Pressed into her mother's shoulder
she breathed what remained.

At 21 she threw her skin off a ferry
        in an old canvas suitcase,
swearing in French at the gale.

The body suit comes out
        at party-time,
still dressed in a hat and fuchsia-pink bra.

Her 35-year-old skin
        wears a thimble,
carries an armful of vinyl.

THE CHANGE

She slid down her own legs,
        squashed the puckered tissue
into a rucksack with their picnic –

at forty-two the moult took seconds
        between sandpit and swings
in Queen's Park.

There were beetle wings
        pencilled on her back,
when the armour fell off.

She felt the draught on her neck.
        Forty-nine – all those times
she could have flown.

Rested, in darkness,
        she hauled herself against a silver birch,
shuddered into the moult.

Her face split at the right eye.
        She scrubbed until the tremor found a fault,
chafed her inside and out.

The shuck was so patched,
        rough with lesions,
she hid it under leaves, crawled away.

WHAT SHE BECAME

Her new skin was watermarked,
       a projection,
almost nothing

to stop womb, liver, lungs
       changing places.
She lay still as it set.

FEMALE ANCESTOR

My

mother's mother's mother's mother's mother's mother's mother's mother's mother's
mother's mother's mother's mother's mother's mother's mother's mother's mother's
mother's mother's mother's mother's mother's mother's mother's mother's mother's
mother's mother's mother's mother's mother's mother's mother's mother's mother's
mother's mother's mother's mother's mother's mother's mother's mother's mother's
mother's mother's mother's mother's mother's mother's mother's mother's mother's
mother's mother's mother's mother's mother's mother's mother's mother's mother's
mother's mother's mother's mother's mother's mother's mother's mother's mother's
mother's mother's mother's mother's mother's mother's mother's mother's mother's
mother's mother's mother's mother's mother's mother's mother's mother's mother's
mother's mother's mother's mother's mother's mother's mother's mother's mother's
mother's mother's mother's mother's mother's mother's mother's mother's mother's
mother's mother's mother's mother's mother's mother's mother's mother's mother's
mother's mother's mother's mother's mother's mother's mother's mother's mother's
mother's mother's mother's mother's mother's mother's mother's mother's mother's
mother's mother's mother's mother's mother's mother's mother's mother's mother's
mother's mother's mother's mother's mother's mother's mother's mother's mother's
mother's mother's mother's mother's mother's mother's mother's mother's mother's
mother's mother's mother's mother's mother's mother's mother's mother's mother's
mother's mother's mother's mother's mother's mother's mother's mother's mother's
mother's mother's mother's mother's mother's mother's mother's mother's mother's
mother's mother's mother's mother's mother's mother's mother's mother's mother's
mother's mother's mother's mother's mother's mother's mother's mother's mother's
mother's mother's mother's mother's mother's mother's mother's mother's mother's
mother's mother's mother's mother's mother's mother's mother's mother's mother's
mother's mother's mother's mother's mother's mother's mother's mother's mother's
mother's mother's mother's mother's mother's mother's mother's mother's mother's
mother's mother's mother's mother's mother's mother's mother's mother's mother's
mother's mother's mother's mother's mother's mother's mother's mother's mother's
mother's mother's mother's mother's mother's mother's mother's mother's mother's
mother's mother's mother's mother's mother's mother's mother's mother's mother's
mother's mother's mother's mother's mother's mother's mother's mother's mother's
mother's mother's mother's mother's mother's mother's mother's mother's mother's
mother's mother's mother's mother's mother's mother's mother's mother's mother's
mother's mother's mother's mother's mother's mother's mother's mother's mother's
mother's mother's mother's mother's mother's mother's mother's mother's mother's
mother's mother's mother's mother's mother's mother's mother's mother's mother's
mother's mother's mother's mother's mother's mother's mother's mother's mother's
mother's mother's mother's mother's mother's mother's mother's mother's mother's
mother's mother's mother's mother's mother's mother's mother's mother's mother's
mother's mother's mother's mother's mother's mother's mother's mother's mother's
mother's mother's mother's mother's mother's mother's mother's mother's mother's
mother's mother's mother's mother's mother's mother's mother's mother's mother's
mother's mother's mother's mother's mother's mother's mother's mother's mother's
mother's mother's mother's mother's mother's mother's mother's mother's mother's
mother's mother's mother's mother's mother's mother's mother's mother's mother's
mother's mother's mother's mother's mother's mother's mother's mother's mother's
mother's mother's mother's mother's mother's mother's mother's mother's mother's

mother.

FIVE AUNTS

balance on the back wall,
a pentatonic scale of legs in nylons,

heels airborne – five faces I could have been.
Even if I'd never seen them in a line,

I'd know them from the distance between nose
and mouth, darkness of their eyes.

Their lips are tracings, their skin my sister's,
mine – each of us is there, times five.

SWEATS

ELEPHANTS

Like killer whales, rhesus monkeys, guppies,
and laboratory mice – elephants experience menopause.

Their symptoms, though, are harder to score
on the Greene Climacteric Scale –

the pressure or tightness in head or body,
attacks of panic, the loss of interest "in most things".

SHE WANTS A BABY

So few or so many men could be carrying
her baby in their hands. She vacuums the clouds
until the storm is overhead, filling
every window of the house.

It escapes to the east, she runs with it
to stand in the column it twists out of the air,
to be with the upturned cars, corrugated iron wings,
to be part of the noise emptying a dirty sky.

IT'S UNCLEAR HOW MUCH OF A MAN SHE NEEDS

Her levels are low.
Is that his smell in the fridge?
It seems she can summon him
from protein. She must eat like a dog.

A WOMAN WITHOUT A MAN

She watches starlings draw a mobius strip
above the pier and decides
a part-time man will do.

WHEN SHE FINDS HERSELF AT THE TOP OF THE STAIRS, SHE BECOMES AN IPOD ON SHUFFLE

There are so many reasons for staring out of a window
counting cars with a bunch of keys in her hand.

LIBIDO

when her skin is not infested with ants
or hives, she discovers that shoreline again

laverbread for breakfast
rioja and chocolate all afternoon

CLOTS

They slide down her toilet like the globs
she scoops from a new tin of emulsion
to slap on the wall.

She'd like to understand this cycle –
her womb lining itself constantly
then having second thoughts.

FOUR PROFESSORS AT THE MENOPAUSE SYMPOSIUM

greet her in their bowties,
four cranes in a river's shallows,
waiting for their wives to return.

Their hypotheses
on bones, memory, sexual dysfunction
and hormone therapy

have made them famous.
They fan her with large wings,
and make a fence

with their long legs. They tap
her with their beaks,
fold themselves around her.

HER BEARD

Under her chin
there's a single sharp hair

that begins as a pimple.
The middle finger of her left hand

knows it.
She can pull it out without a mirror.

How would it look, the beard
she won't permit?

SPIDERS HAVE PLACED A CATAPLASM OF WEBS

over her head that renews itself
whenever she paints it away

SMEAR

Perhaps the cells in mucus on the tip of a spatula
could be grown into an alternative version
of herself?

HYPOTHALAMUS

When the blowtorch is on inside her
and she's throwing bricks at windows for air
she hooks herself into the national grid
to supply the city's tumble dryers.

SUPERANNUATION

Her fingers have become kindling.
They cannot twist a button
as if the thought of decoration repels them.

When she needs to sew, her right hand
refuses to feel. At the window
she mimes the arms-length threading

of cotton and eye, mimes embroidery –
at the edge of numbness,
a border of spills.

HER MIRROR FACE IS SPINNING

showing how deep and expertly
each line is nicked into her skin.

VEINS

A purple tattoo large as a hand
is doodled across her right thigh.

And the M1, with twisting A-roads,
has appeared on her shins,
a mountain track behind one knee.

HER TROUBLES

The hushed vocabulary
blooms with micro-organisms,
prolapse, dyspareunia.

HER HEART

The thrush with a broken neck
is still warm when the cat brings it to her.
Her heart is behaving like a cat.

TRACE

Her cheek fizzed. She felt it tug.
It was the gentlest of strokes,
a voice deflected by wind shear,
a slow-worm crossing the lawn.

ATROPHY

She crouches and tilts
a magnifying mirror
to examine the fissures
that have appeared in her flesh.

Unlike the moon,
whose rilles
were magnificent rivers of lava,
she is eroding.

IV

RETURN

The third time I wake, it's light and shouldn't be.
Someone outside is grunting – regular, timed breaths,

he's jogging uphill, balancing two shovels
on his shoulder. I know him by sight, his eyes

show only the run, a Death Valley marathon.
He trains in boots. The definition of his arms,

the shine on his head come from sweat –
like the trophies my grandfather won in nine,

ten rounds in so many provincial boxing rings.
And so it's Thomas Harte who comes to mind

when I stare up the road at this man's back –
the name I go online for, searching Irish

Censuses repeatedly, scanning for a shoemaker
in Dublin, who will step forward and identify

himself as the father of my mother's father,
holding his awl, a skiver, his leather knife,

who'll last the family's halves together,
peg her present to his past, sole to hide.

IMAGINING MY GREAT GRANDMOTHER

My mother's hair – so thick
her eyes deep set,

unpierced ears
and small, square fingernails,

big toes pointing north-west, north-east,
a weakness for clairvoyants.

She has my mother's need
to push her hands in soil, believes in hauntings.

She wears scarves in navy and green,
a knotted rope of pearls.

What do I call her? Will she hear her name
if I list what's in this window –

sycamore, dog rose, nettle, pigeon,
the damselfly hovering round the stream?

THE AIR ON LEWES ROAD

Let the air remember how it was when wives lugged the catch
to Lewes on the fish route, the road glinting with scales
as if time itself was in their baskets among the herring.

Let the viaduct reassemble arch by arch
and the Level bonfire reignite to consume its effigies.

Let the air resurrect the Bernard Oppenheimer Diamond Works
for amputees, the pill factory, Reverend Wagner's home for prostitutes,
the pease pudding and faggot shop.

Let the silent film stars return to the old Arcadia –
Mae Murray in Altars of Desire, Molly Malone in The Soul Herder.

Let the air genuflect at the altar of St Martin's
designed by H. Ellis Wooldridge,
with its 69 statues carved in Oberammergau.

Let us kneel to the dead carried to the crematorium
by Ray Trafford of Skinners, my aunt among them.

Let the air feed poets Albert E. Coppard,
New Elizabethan, and Brendan Cleary of Bear Road,
the gyratory village and the Gladstone.

Let the elms breathe the same air as in the beginning
when lines of saplings pledged magnificent avenues.

Let the air scatter into pavement cracks, parking bays,
blue as borage, morning glory, delphiniums,
forget-me-nots, creeping bellflower, self-heal.

THE KITCHEN FLOOR

This is how I spend my afternoons,
settle my calves, buttocks and shoulders
on the kitchen floor, cushioned by the quiet
of empty cups and stacked plates.
There is nothing to do but sleep.

This is the floor I sweep and mop,
where I stand and cook.
I lie in my shadow's space.
Only the clock moves
and the bacteria on my skin.

I lie in a rectangle of sun.
The large window's open,
cats might come and go.
I lie in the centre of the paths I've worn
from door to sink, worktop to oven.

I am big as a mixing bowl,
even the baby inside me is sleeping.
Objections slam the front door as they leave.
I'm an elderly primigravida
with my head on the floorboards.

I can feel the whole house through the joists
and the terrace curving back on itself
under the viaduct as a train waits above me
for a signal to cross.
I am settling into photo albums,

stepping out of dresses I can't give away.
I am moving the furniture, choosing my places.

Lovely came to us like that –
sat on the windowsill with her black and ginger face
and wouldn't leave.

When I wake up,
I'll see the dust under the fridge,
grease on the cooker's hidden sides.
Until then the floor is cool and I am still
as a white teapot on a shelf beside a white jug.

DIRTY BUSINESS

Jam-jars of screws are thrown into the van,
Barbara's sewing machine, John's car manuals,

half an exhaust pipe, swivel chair, three rusty saws.
With each crash I want to run next door.

Four lads and a girl from Dirty Business are tipping
the house into the garden. Paper, wood, metal, glass –

as Barbara did when words went missing.
On this forecourt every summer, they aired the trailer tent.

The street listens to a mallet shatter mirrors,
bolts fire from a tin – and a wind picks up the inventory.

THE DAY BEFORE HE LEFT

It was behind the glass, shivering,
eyes fixed on me,
as far into the corner of the window-well as it could get.

I was in the cellar, it had fallen down from the lawn
and I wondered, at first,
if it had already eaten the young frog I'd seen a week before.

I went into the garden to free it
and it looked up at me, screaming. Giya and her friend looked,
it screamed at them and they screamed back.

Last year a fox cub fell in and I wrapped it in a blanket,
released it in the cemetery.
But what could I do with a rat?

Since the Tribe of Doris summer camp in 2008
and Olu's guided journey to find the animal within,
I wondered what made my body remember itself as a rat.

On my last birthday, a rat sauntered across the kitchen
as if it lived with me.
The rodent man said it was most likely an opportunist.

Now, on the day before my first born moves out,
before I drive him to a run-down house, leave him with strangers,
the rat looks at me through the cellar window and I look back.

LANDLORD VISITING THE STUDENT QUARTER

Welcome the sovereign of bedrooms who'll fill the vacuum
of your nights with a house of girls roaring into shot glasses.

Stop him on the corner of Baxter Street where a mattress
is folded in a front garden, two doors up from a broken divan.

He's surely a man creative with bricks and plasterboard?
See the orange of spores on the back of the mirror.

When it rains he becomes a waterfall in a chimney, draining
into earth below the kitchen you once joked held bones.

He coils himself into flex, breaks himself down to settle
as grease on a shelf. He installs a web in the smoke alarm.

And on his way up your hill, that he's buying metre by metre,
he turns into September, when houses are let, chairs become kindling.

He chains bikes to lampposts till they rust back to ore.
Know him from his car, the keys he carries in wash-bags.

You won't find his number. He's discrete as the woodlice
he keeps on the ceiling. But visit his shrine in the mattress shop –

offer your Yale as an amulet, a KFC bucket, light a candle
perfumed with vinegar, cigarette smoke and lager, base notes

of Lloyd Grossman, ripe banana. You may leave a relic –
a twist of fuse wire perhaps – and many will pray here.

SANDWICH MAN ADVERTISING PIZZA

Free garlic bread.

Meat Machine and Sizzler,
my DAY OF JUDGEMENT specials.

I stand between two pizzas at the lights,
mascot of binmen filling the void.

RECOVERING YOU

When my neighbour describes the new rhythm
of her son's heart, its speed, its extra note,
I think of you on a treadmill and warfarin.

And when mine's galloping because I've seen that wine
you like, I wonder if your heart has lodged itself again
inside one of my four chambers. It might explain

why remnants of you, stored in my hair and skin,
still assemble to recover you. Why walking
on the racecourse in fog this afternoon

I was counting the pulse of two bass and treble horns –
one from the marina every fifteen seconds,
one answering from the invisible sea.

STOLEN IDENTITY

To John Windsor who uses my address
for a Screwfix account and Max Miller
who's never lived here but does according to Virgin,

to the unknown person who swiped my card
three times in New York and twice in Boston,
I say, come and live with me

behind the cemetery with a cat, wren,
teenagers and all I never learned.
Take my name from the bills I forgot to burn,

detach it from the dubious ancestors
and we'll share out futures – I can be a physicist,
I can be a carpenter.

Float this name into the Amazon,
fly it over the walls of Lewes prison,
let the storks of Marrakesh line their nests with it.

If you need it to rent a car or tv – it's yours.
Come in the way the sun does,
tell me all I've done –

the Ducatti I rode pillion, verges I stood on,
the stained glass door with cracks in
I come back to every day.

SHEEPCOTE VALLEY

Today the first elder is out,
creamy, narcotic.

The dog's disturbed a skylark
and this will go on all summer.

I watch the bird hurl itself up,
away from an invisible nest.

It beats a vertical song
a thousand feet high

and disappears into
two hundred and thirty notes

a second, amplifies
earth and sun.

The lark claims me,
the dog walker with his pack,

the boy with no job, trying Asda again.
It shakes out the sky

and smooths the sea
to catch whoever falls.

GYRATORY

On Friday nights the cycle lane disappears
beneath a line of waiting cars outside Wine Me Up,
Booze Factor and Perfect Pizza. Men criss-cross
the pavement with padded bags and cool boxes.
You can always buy a beer on Lewes Road.
And when the cycle lane appears again, the cyclist
looks towards the gyratory. She knows the gyratory
has its own rules, governed by a stranded pub
and petrol station. Not even Sainsbury's has influence –
customers backed up into the car park, refused entry.
More than a crossroads, cars meet from six directions,
split off into seven lanes – left to Five Ways, Lewes,
up the hill of death, into a dead end or round again –
to town, to town, to town. On the gyratory, the cyclist
tenses her arms, looks straight ahead. The rope
she balances both tyres on is held between poles
by enormous carabiners. She must ignore the 49b
revving behind her, the Big Yellow breathing out
chip fumes, the concrete mixer, silver van.
She cannot think of herself as flesh on the gyratory,
where the cycle lane no longer exists. She must be as sure
as time that it will reappear just after Shabitat,
the second hand superstore. She must be as sure
as faith, as the AtoZ or a 24 hour delivery man.

FUNERAL HORSES

They stamp the yellow lines outside
the cemetery's pink stone columns.
A horsebox is waiting, they drink in turns
from a water bucket offered by the groom.
One nuzzles her armpit,
another shakes his white flash, they snort.

It was a double funeral today – two
black pairs and the percussion of sixteen hooves
carried two pale coffins,
rosebuds wired into hearts,
white chrysanths twice mouthing SON.
They've obeyed the slightest tension in a rein

and with their sixteen hooves ushered two families
from home, past Moulsecoomb Primary,
the library, derelict TA centre, university,
past CarpetRight and Halfords, The Gladstone…
slowing Lewes Road to a shuffle –
hushing it with their shoes and feathers.

And everyone on foot, in a bus or car stopped –
their own dead brought to attention beside them.
The horses turned at Skinners to climb the hill,
delivered their loads to the chapel,
carried them again to the graves.
Now the groom brushes each one down,

smooths their necks, running her right hand
over their backs. She untethers them one by one
from iron railings, buckles coats on to lead them
into the horsebox. The hearses are gone. She murmurs,
they nod, she puts her hand to their mouths,
they take a slice of apple, lick salt from her palm.

BIOGRAPHICAL NOTE

JACKIE WILLS has published three collections of poetry with Arc Publications: *Powder Tower* (1995), *Fever Tree* (2003), *Commandments* (2007) and one with Leviathan: *Party* (2000). *Powder Tower* was a Poetry Book Society Recommendation and Wills was shortlisted for the 1995 T.S. Eliot prize. In 2004, *Mslexia* magazine named her one of the 10 new woman poets of the decade.

Born in Wiltshire, Wills now lives in Brighton. She was Royal Literary Fund Fellow at the universities of Surrey and Sussex between 2009 and 2012.

Selected titles in Arc Publications'
POETRY FROM THE UK / IRELAND include: